Throug
Magic Window

Written by Corinna Shepherd
Illustrated by Ciaran Finnegan

This book belongs to

....

Published by Dancing Kites Publishing

Dedications

To the children at the Chilterns IDL (Dyslexia) Centre,
who helped and inspired me to write this book.

My thanks to countless people, who have offered support, advice and
kept me going, including family, friends and business associates.

First published in 2010 by Dancing Kites Publishing
www.dancingkites.co.uk

ISBN 978-1-907706-02-8

Design & production by Pagewise
www.pagewise.co.uk

Granny on a motorbike
Speeding through the town

Wearing goggles and a hat
And a flowing gown

1

Pick me up and come with me
I want to fly above the tree

Grab my string and let me go
I want to dance high – fast and slow

I catch the wind to get me high
Instead I dive down with a sigh

I'm lifted up and look around
A rush of wind my only sound

Now I dance, now I am free
High in the sky **for all to see!**

2

Through the magic window
Take a look and see

Far off lands and places
Explore them all with me

A hamster and a unicorn
A **giant** in the sky

Floating on a sunbeam
All kinds of things
to spy

4

The invisible man
ran down the street

Red socks and shoes
upon his feet

He ran right past me
at high speed

Scared a man with a
dog on a lead

So how do we know
if he's **big** or small?

He left a **big dent**,
where he hit the wall

The **giant** flung a jar of stars
Across the midnight sky

The patterns made were prettier
Than a painting you could buy

Reflected in a magic lake
A copy of the sky

I dive right in and float along
And watch the world go by

Waiting at the starting line
all desperate to win
A **penguin** in a satin skin
with a violin

A **robin** and a **goblin**
longing to begin
A **dolphin** with a pumpkin
balanced on its fin

A **puffin** eating a muffin
and making a loud din
Which one is the fastest?
Who do you think
will win?

I float up in a bubble

Higher than the moon

I want to get to outer space

And hope I get there soon

I float on past a rocket

And drift above a star

Sitting in my see-through sphere

I've really travelled far

12

Find the hidden words and circle them.

j	i	l	s	b	u	b	b	l	e	j	w
u	v	g	p	s	p	h	e	r	e	i	e
y	q	o	e	t	d	o	l	p	h	i	n
n	d	w	e	f	w	z	g	i	d	n	r
r	x	n	d	p	e	n	g	u	i	n	u
i	n	v	i	s	i	b	l	e	j	s	o
o	z	i	e	g	v	d	a	n	c	e	e
y	n	l	c	s	r	o	c	k	e	t	i
u	m	i	d	n	i	g	h	t	s	x	f
z	x	x	z	p	h	m	k	f	v	j	f
z	m	r	u	d	x	l	e	a	d	u	p
y	f	s	g	o	g	g	l	e	s	o	e

bubble   goggles   lead   rocket
dance   gown   midnight   speed
dolphin   invisible penguin   sphere

Thank you for your purchase. I am sure you and the child in your life will enjoy your new book.

Now that you have made your first purchase, perhaps you would like to stay in touch so you can be the first to know when subsequent titles are coming out.

To join our mailing list, visit www.dancingkites.co.uk and click on the Subscribe to our email newsletter button at the bottom right of the page.

Another way to keep in touch is **to visit my blog** at www.blog.dancingkites.co.uk/, where you can find out the latest on the Dancing Kites brand, what Corinna's up to and comments and links to matters relating to dyslexia. Can you afford to miss it?

Follow me on Twitter: www.twitter.com/CorinnaShepherd

Can you help?

The lines of the poem have got muddled up. Can you sort them out so the race can begin?

RACE DAY.

A penguin in a satin skin

longing to begin

A robin and a goblin

and making a loud din

A dolphin with a pumpkin

with a violin

A puffin eating a muffin

balanced on its fin

Who do you want to win?

Through the magic window
Take another look

Different scenes before your eyes
Like pictures in a book

A **princess** in a castle
Waiting for her **knight**

A **scary dragon** breathing fire
And **goblins** in a fight

16

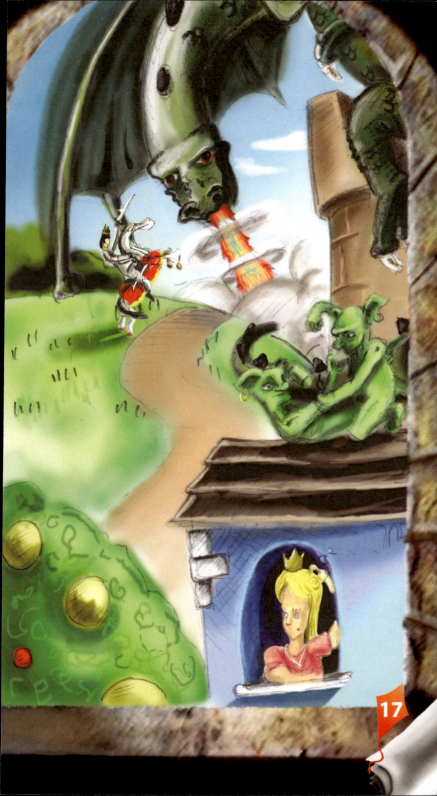

I rode upon a **hamster** small
It went too fast – we had a fall

I rode upon a **unicorn**
All through the night until the dawn

18

I rode upon a **rattlesnake**
I think that was a big mistake

But **best of all** I rode a bird
That was the ride that I preferred

19

I have a *secret* cupboard
Hidden deep within my house

It's opened with a **magic key**
And guarded by a **mouse**

No-one else has found it yet
What things are kept in there?

Let's put the key into the lock
And open – **if you dare!**

The invisible man

– he sat on my chair

And as I walked past

he tugged on my hair

The invisible man

– he ate beans on toast

But is he a man or

is he a **ghost?**

Home
Sweet
Home

23

Find the hidden words and circle them

w	o	s	e	c	r	e	t	y	g	s	k
e	z	n	z	r	e	h	d	b	i	r	d
n	h	g	b	u	a	c	p	l	g	r	v
l	w	p	i	c	t	u	r	e	s	b	y
r	a	t	t	l	e	s	n	a	k	e	h
y	o	j	u	g	e	h	j	d	o	q	a
d	k	d	n	l	k	n	i	g	h	t	i
r	t	h	r	o	u	g	h	h	e	u	r
a	t	i	o	c	u	p	b	o	a	r	d
g	d	i	r	c	t	y	i	u	k	o	a
o	z	o	o	m	o	u	s	e	d	s	w
n	h	e	k	n	i	g	h	t	v	e	n

bird   dragon   mouse   rattlesnak

cupboard   hair   night   secret

dawn   knight   pictures   through

24

Through
the magic window...
What can you see?

Fill in the gaps from the
Through the magic window poems

A h_ _ st_ r and a _ _ _ co_ n

A g_ _ nt in the sk_

A pri_ _ _ ss in a ca_ _ le

A sca_ _ dr_ g_ n breathing f_ re

G_ b_ _ ns in a fi_ _ t

What else can YOU see?
Write down below

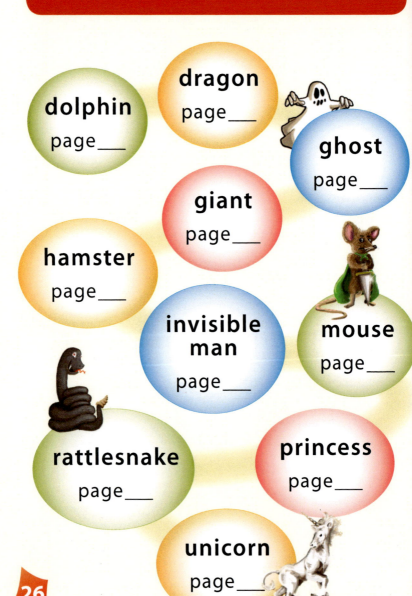

dolphin
page___

dragon
page___

ghost
page___

giant
page___

hamster
page___

invisible man
page___

mouse
page___

rattlesnake
page___

princess
page___

unicorn
page___